To

_____

On the Occasion of

_____

From

_____

GOD'S FRONT DOOR

Private Conversations

JILL BRISCOE

MONARCH
BOOKS

Oxford, UK & Grand Rapids, Michigan

First published in the UK in 2004 by Monarch Books,
(a publishing imprint of Lion Hudson plc),
Wilkinson House, Jordan Hill Road, Oxford OX2 8DR.
Tel: +44 (0) 1865 302750 Fax: +44 (0) 1865 302757
monarch@lionhudson.com
www.lionhudson.com

Reprinted 2009, 2010.

Distributed by:
UK: Marston Book Services Ltd, PO Box 269, Abingdon, Oxford OX14 4YN;
USA: Kregel Publications, PO Box 2607, Grand Rapids, Michigan 49501.

ISBN: 978 1 85424 641 7 (UK)
ISBN: 978 0 8254 6010 7 (USA)

Unless otherwise indicated, Scripture quotations are taken from
the *Holy Bible, New International Version*, © 1973, 1978, 1984 by the International Bible
Society. Used by permission of Hodder and Stoughton Ltd. Scripture quotations marked
NLT are taken from the *Holy Bible*, New Living Translation, copyright © 1996.
Used by permission of Tyndale House Publishers, Inc.,
Wheaton, Illinois 60189. All rights reserved.

Photography: Bill Bain, Alan Bedding, Dave Cooke, Roger Chouler,
Alison Hickey, Glyn Simister Lewis, Donna Pendrey.

British Library Cataloguing Data
A catalogue record for this book is available from the British Library.

Printed and bound in China by Printplus Ltd.

TO RUTH GRAHAM,

WITH LOVE AND GRATITUDE

FOR ALWAYS ENCOURAGING ME

TO REACH HIGHER,

STRETCH THE SIDES OF MY SOUL,

AND GO FOR THE GOLD!

CONTENTS

COMMENDATION

*A*LL MY LIFE I HAVE loved poetry, and since I have come to know Jill, I have come to love her. So the combination for me is unbeatable.

It is a privilege to recommend this book for your pleasure, enrichment and inspiration.

Ruth Bell Graham
USA
July 2003

A WORD FROM THE AUTHOR

I WAS EIGHTEEN YEARS OF AGE, attending a teachers' training college in Cambridge, England, trying to figure out the world, and looking for a reason for which to live and die. Someone gave me a book to read by C. S. Lewis.

Churchless and godless, I read it and was introduced to a whole new world. I began to devour this man's writings, little knowing he was at Cambridge too! He of course was a distinguished professor, I a little student staggering towards truth. As I wrote recently in an essay on Lewis: "It was Lewis' book *The Weight of Glory* that made heaven not only believable, but also attainable through the Christ who was the love of Lewis' life after years as an atheist and a formidable antagonist to all things Christian."

Lewis writes: "At present we are on the outside of the world, the wrong side of the door. We cannot mingle with the splendours we see. But all the leaves of the New Testament are rustling with the rumour that it will not always be so. Some day, God willing, we shall get 'in'" (p. 13). And again: "A cleft has

AT PRESENT WE ARE ON THE OUTSIDE OF THE WORLD, THE WRONG SIDE OF THE DOOR. WE CANNOT MINGLE WITH THE SPLENDOURS WE SEE.

opened in the pitiless walls of the world, and we are invited to follow our great Captain inside. Glory!" (p. 15).

This image of being on the "wrong side" of the door I one day will "get in", has sown within me a desire to share some of my soul's discoveries as I have sat on the steps and talked to, listened to, and conversed with the Jesus who is my Saviour and Lord, the love of my life, my reason for being and my highest joy.

I invite you to sit on the steps with me, and share some intimate "soul talk", trusting this will stimulate some conversations of your own.

THIS IMAGE OF BEING ON

THE "WRONG SIDE" OF

THE DOOR I ONE DAY

WILL "GET IN", HAS SOWN

WITHIN ME A DESIRE TO

SHARE SOME OF MY

SOUL'S DISCOVERIES.

FEARS
AND
TROUBLE

TURBULENCE

"YOU WILL NOT FEAR THE TERROR OF NIGHT,
NOR THE ARROW THAT FLIES BY DAY."
Psalm 91: 5

*A*RE YOU AFRAID OF FLYING? I USED TO BE. People are anxious about it especially now when airport security reminds you of things that could go wrong on even a short flight.

When I first came to the USA over thirty years ago I was terrified to get on a plane. One day I was sitting looking over my notes on a flight when the plane ran into severe weather. My heart gave a lurch. I tried to concentrate on my notes.

I was to address a large audience on the subject of faith! It was obviously time to talk to the Lord. My mind ran to the Psalms and parked on Psalm 91: 5. "You will not fear the terror of night, nor the arrow that flies by day." The Captain's voice jolted me out of my thoughts, "Fasten your seat belts, we are experiencing some turbulence." I hated this. My heart rate increased.

I glanced across the aisle and jumped. He was sitting in the seat opposite me. I noticed He had His seat belt on. "That's funny," I said, "You've got Your seat belt fastened."

"It's good to obey the rules," He said.

"Is it going to be that bad?" I asked apprehensively. He laughed.

"I hate flying," I said.

"Better than riding a donkey," He remarked. "And safer!"

"I think it's to do with flying through the devil's territory," I continued.

"You mean because he is the prince of the power of the air?" He asked me.

"Yes."

"He's the prince, but I'm the King," He replied.

"We're so high up," I said looking apprehensively out of the window.

"You're nearer The Front Door up here," He responded cheerfully.

Then I was "really" nervous! I didn't want to hurt His feelings so I didn't say anything else. I glanced sideways to see if He knew what I was thinking. His eyes were twinkling. He knew, of course. I knew He knew. Who was I kidding?

"Lord, it's not that I don't want to live with You forever, it's just… just… " (He didn't help me out.) "It's just – I wasn't expecting it to be *today*," I finished lamely. He laughed again and the plane gave a lurch

"LORD, IT'S NOT THAT I DON'T WANT TO LIVE WITH YOU FOREVER, IT'S JUST…JUST…IT'S JUST – I WASN'T EXPECTING IT TO BE *TODAY.*"

Fears and Trouble

and a bump and another bump and I reached across the aisle and caught hold of His hand.

"This is fun," He said cheerfully. "So much better than a donkey." He should know!

And then I wasn't frightened any more. Maybe it was because I was thinking about Psalm 91: 5, "You shall not be afraid for... the arrow that flies by day." Was "this" the arrow that flies by day, I wondered? I sort of knew the arrow in the Psalm was a wooden one, while this arrow was metal, but the verse helped me to calm down. After all, He was on board.

I looked around the cabin. Did the stewardess know He was in seat 10A, I wondered? Should I tell her? I decided to wait and see what happened when they offered Him a coke.

Then the plane began to land, and glancing sideways I realized He had taken a short cut home and was gone. Gathering up my notes, I began to look forward to my faith talk. Now I had something to say!

Lord of the heavens and the earth,

make me brave. Nerve my will to

trust You with this lump of metal I'm

riding in as we hurtle through the

clouds. Help my theology to help me.

Give me peace of mind and

thankfulness for quick ways to get to

the places You are sending me to in

order to serve You. It's time I grew up.

I'm ready; show me how. Love, Jill.

HOT WATER

"Yet I am always with You;
You hold me by my right hand."
Psalm 73: 23

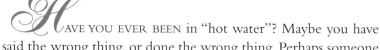

Have you ever been in "hot water"? Maybe you have said the wrong thing, or done the wrong thing. Perhaps someone took offence at your sincere effort to mediate in a dispute. All of us have been in this uncomfortable place sometimes in our lives!

I was thinking about this as I made a cup of tea – tea bag style – and climbed the hill to The Front Door. I thought maybe He would join me, though I didn't think He drank tea – certainly not if it was made with a tea bag instead of the "real" way! After all, everyone knows that God is an Englishman!

It was quiet and I played with the steaming water and watched the little tea bag doing its own thing – MMMM it smelled so good.

I felt sorry for the tea bag really. I knew what it was like to be in hot water – but, oh, the aroma! The thought caught my imagination. After all, I had been in plenty of hot water in my time.

There was the time I arrived in India and found I had

arrived at the same time as the bubonic plague broke out. Actually it started in the very town I was in!

Then I thought about being on United Flight 929 high over the Atlantic, on 11 September 2001 – not a good idea. Next I remembered the time I made a bad decision in ministry – and everyone was mad at me – for months. And I thought about more than a couple of speeding tickets I had acquired! Hot water!

I looked at The Front Door, but it remained fast shut, so I took out my pencil and a scrap of paper and began to pen a letter to leave on The Door for Him. It didn't take me long.

Am I like a tea bag waiting to know
What flavour I am when in hot H_2O?

Am I like a tea bag, soggy and wet?
Am I asking the Lord just how hot it can get?

I want to be able to give out for sure
A fragrant aroma that makes folks want more –

But that means hot water that hurts my deep pride
That cleans out my life 'til I'm tired inside,
Of a fragrant-less life, that knows not how to sing –
So dip me in water, BUT KEEP HOLD OF THE
    STRING!
Love, Jill.

I scribbled an RSVP on the bottom and a few days later found my poem gone and the reply pinned on The Front Door.

"Nice poem – will do it."

I think about this every time I make myself a cup of tea.

Lord, I so often get myself into hot

water. I know the aroma of Your

presence in my life is evident at these

times. People tell me so,

so I suppose it is true.

But I don't like it one little bit. But

this I know – You "always" keep

hold of the string!

Thank You – You are the best!

Love, Jill.

GOD'S FRONT DOOR

$\mathscr{P}$RIORITIES

INTERRUPTIONS

"WHAT YOU OUGHT TO SAY IS: 'IF THE LORD WANTS US TO, WE
WILL LIVE AND DO THIS AND THAT.'"
James 4: 15 (NLT)

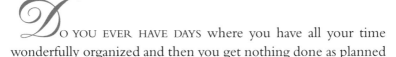

*D*O YOU EVER HAVE DAYS where you have all your time wonderfully organized and then you get nothing done as planned because of constant interruptions?

It was at the end of such a day that I carried my complaints to The Front Door, and sat down. I couldn't wait for Him to come, but The Door was shut and He didn't immediately appear. I was irritated because my day had been full of interruptions and I couldn't wait to start griping about it.

A thought occurred to me that I had come to complain about all my interruptions, but I was going to interrupt *Him* doing whatever He was doing! Well, I reasoned, that was different! It was His job to drop everything and attend to me!

I began to think about my messy day. I had had it all scheduled out and then it began. I no sooner got going when the phone rang, the kids called, the washing machine overflowed, the dog ran away, and a needy person appeared from nowhere and demanded my attention. I hate that!

The needy lady didn't fare too well! I tried to listen to her litany of woes, but I had my eye on the clock and she caught me glancing at it every two minutes! She left hurriedly, feeling unwelcome, uncared for, unloved, and as empty as she came. I felt a twinge of guilt, but thankfully it soon passed, hurried out the door of my conscience by all my righteous excuses.

"Well," I assured myself – "It was her fault! She hadn't made an appointment!"

"I made one for her" a voice said in my ear! I jumped – I hadn't seen Him arrive. "You made the appointment?" I asked as if He was speaking so quietly I couldn't quite hear Him! (He knows I'm a little deaf.) And then I blurted out – "But You didn't check with me first!"

"You didn't check with Me either," He pointed out mildly, sitting down. I noticed He had some plans in His hands.

I managed to peek surreptitiously at the papers. They looked incredibly complicated. Had I interrupted some grand cosmic meeting where the Trinity was looking at creating a few more universes? Now that was a scary thought!

"What's the matter?" He asked kindly.

I began my litany of woes. I talked for at least twenty minutes without stopping. After all I had had a lot of interruptions and I wanted to make sure I complained about every single one of them!

I suddenly noticed He had not looked at His world-watch once! He was just sitting there and I knew I was centre stage in

I SUDDENLY NOTICED HE HAD

NOT LOOKED AT HIS WORLD-

WATCH ONCE!

HE WAS JUST SITTING THERE AND I

KNEW I WAS CENTRE STAGE

IN HIS THINKING!

His thinking! I thought about the grand cosmic plans in His hands, and then I thought about all my petty little gripes. The worried woman's face appeared in my mind and I tried hard to ignore it. What had He said? That "He" had made the appointment for her?

"She needed you," He said simply, following my thoughts.

"But Lord – You know what my schedule looked like!" I argued.

"You had a choice," He replied. "It's really quite simple. People matter more than schedules, Jill. When I lived outside The Front Door, I was constantly interrupted by the multitude, but I believed my Heavenly Father made My day and He knew He could interrupt it as He wished."

"Oh," I muttered miserably.

He didn't pat me on the head and say, "There, there – it doesn't really matter", or hit me over the head with a verse from His Book. He just sat there. I looked at Him carefully. Then I noticed He was praying. I didn't want to interrupt that so I stayed very still. I felt very uncomfortable because I was certain He was praying for me.

When He stopped I said, "Thank You, Lord, for praying for me!"

"I wasn't," he replied calmly. "I was praying for her! The woman I sent to interrupt you." Now I was speechless. (Well, that was a start.)

He left then. I got to my feet and reached out to Him and He turned at The Door and looked right through me and I knew He was looking right at my heart.

"Is it hard?" I whispered.

"Yes," He said.

"Soften it Lord – please!"

"All right."

"Please Lord, if it's not too late, send her back to me tomorrow."

"But your schedule's already full of things to do."

"Please Lord – I'll be waiting."

There was a long silence. He was gone.

She didn't come back – why should she? What did I miss that day? Who else received the blessing of investing in her life? What a loss.

Lord God, would You in Your grace forgive me?

In Your mercy make me like Your sweet Son.

In Your love, grant me another day to

love the people You send my way.

May they not be disappointed.

Interrupt my pettiness with things of

eternal importance. Teach me to allow You to

fill my calendar. Grant me another day

and another way to live.

GOD'S FRONT DOOR

GET THEM IN ONES

"DO NOT WORRY ABOUT TOMORROW,
FOR TOMORROW WILL WORRY ABOUT ITSELF.
EACH DAY HAS ENOUGH TROUBLE OF ITS OWN."
Matthew 6: 34

Do YOU EVER RUN OUT OF strength, grit, and determination? Do you panic when tomorrow looks dark and impossible? I understand. Many times I have a knot in my stomach as I look at the things I have said "yes" to, and wonder just how on earth it is all going to get done. There are times when my laid-back husband is a huge help to me, and there are times when I can't do what he suggests. Then I know it's time to go to The Front Door.

"Father, Stuart is such a challenge to me. He always says the strengthening thing, just when I'm panicking about something or other!"

"That's what husbands are for."

> MANY TIMES I HAVE A KNOT
> IN MY STOMACH AS I LOOK
> AT THE THINGS
> I HAVE SAID "YES" TO,
> AND WONDER JUST HOW ON
> EARTH IT IS ALL GOING TO
> GET DONE.

Priorities

"But I think he's the BEST HUSBAND. I think he's perfect for me. Thank You, thank You, he's mine!"

"You're welcome."

"I want to be strengthening for him too, but he never panics. He likes to hear me say 'I love you' though."

"Even though you've been married 45 years?"

"Yes."

"That's good, and that's what wives are for – to say, 'I love you.' That's strengthening! So, what did he say about you overloading again?"

"As if You don't know!"

"Let's talk about it."

"That's what prayer is about, isn't it, Lord? Talking to You even when You know all the stuff already."

"Yes."

"Well, You know how my stomach goes into a knot when I've taken so much on."

"Oh, yes."

"Like when I was packing to go and face seven meetings in two days (and that's just the speaking without the four meal meetings scheduled). And then I knew there would be people who would want to have a talk with me about their problems in between."

"There are a lot of problems out there."

"Well, as I kissed Stuart goodbye and said, 'Pray for me,' he put his arms around me (I love it when he does that) and asked what I would be facing. He listened carefully (I love it when he does that), and said 'Get them in ones!'

"I knew what he meant at once. He was talking 'cricket' wasn't he? You know about cricket, Lord?"

His eyes twinkled so I knew He did! "When you're down in a match and have to get runs and it's tempting to use energy and take risks swinging for the boundary." Amazing. God even knows about cricket!

"Well, it's hard not to go all out when you've got to get the job done. Especially when you are up against something formidable," I said somewhat defensively.

"Get them in ones," Stuart repeated. "One by one by one, hour by hour by hour, minute by minute by minute. Take it a run at a time." Then he added, "You only have to take seven meetings? That's only three and a half a day!"

"I hate it when he does that," I complained. "He's such a numbers man!"

The Lord laughed then, not at me (never at me), but with me.

"No, you don't hate it, you love it. Stuart's a good man, He's 'My' man – and yours."

Then it was time to go, and I walked out of my front door of opportunity, picking up my cricket bat on the way. And I thought about how each time I walk out of my own front door into my daily days of service, I am a few steps nearer His. That felt good!

Dear Father, this is a difficult match. The other team is ahead.

Help me to walk out onto the pitch of the day,

hold my head up high and win each match for You.

Help me to "get them in ones".

Priorities

LIFE
AND
SERVICE

DISAPPOINTMENT

"O unbelieving and perverse generation...
how long shall I stay with you?
How long shall I put up with you?"
Matthew 17: 17

Have you ever had it with people? Perhaps you've been disappointed with those you've left in charge, who you thought would come through for you? Have they left you to pick up the pieces when your plate was already overloaded? Have they let you down? Have you ever just wanted to throw up your hands and go home? I have. It's best to go and talk it over when you feel like that. He knows all about the burden that weighs you down. He'll help you deal with it and move on.

I wanted to talk to Him about being disappointed with people. I found Him waiting for me in a shady place just around the corner of The Front Door.

"Hullo."

"Hullo."

"Did You ever want out?" I asked, knowing He knew why I'd come.

"Yes."

"When?"

"After the Mount of Transfiguration, when I came down from the mountain top and found a child needing help and My disciples helpless."

I remembered the story. A small boy devastated by a demon, and the impotent disciples. Men who "could not", as the Bible said. They "could not" trust enough, "could not" pray enough and "could not" cast out a demon in the power of Jesus Christ. They had cast demons out before, but not this time, and so they just waited for Jesus to come down from the mountain top and do it.

Then I remembered He had said to His faithless men, "How long must I suffer you?"

"But You didn't go home, did You?" I asked.

"I hadn't finished My work," He said simply.

We were quiet for a bit. I too was fed up with some people who were leaving me to do it all. I was tired of serving the church.

"I want to go home and I haven't finished mine either!" I replied. "People are driving me up the wall – sapping my strength with so many demands. They don't finish what they start. They know I'll end up picking up the bits and doing it for them." He didn't say anything.

"It wears on you," I said. I was getting weary with all my griping.

I TOO WAS FED UP WITH SOME PEOPLE WHO WERE LEAVING ME TO DO IT ALL. I WAS TIRED OF SERVING THE CHURCH.

41

"Complaining tires me out," I complained. Silence.

"Oh, all right, how do I get it all done?"

"Start with the attitude," He said mildly. "I did always those things that pleased the Father, so I healed the boy, finished other people's tasks, and kept on walking towards Jerusalem."

"What kept You going?"

"You did! I thought of you, Jill, and how one day you and I would have this talk and I'd be able to tell you, 'Just do it tired!' Do your work till every single piece of it is done. Do it for Me and do it again and again until you walk right through The Front Door at the end of the day. There will be plenty of time to rest in eternity!"

We laughed then. "How can there be plenty of time in eternity?" I asked.

"Trust Me," he replied. "I can make everything needful there. One day you will burn on brightly forever. No more burnout on the other side of The Front Door."

THERE IS NOTHING THAT WEARIES YOU MORE THAN A COMPLAINING SPIRIT.

I went back then – to pick up the bits and finish other people's jobs – with a better attitude. There is nothing that wearies you more than a complaining spirit.

"My word says, 'when I complained, my spirit was overwhelmed!'" I heard Him call after me!

Lord, make me like Jesus – burning
on without burning out. Deal with
my attitude when I'm fed up and
disappointed with people. And give
me grace to get the job done!

Life and Service

WORDS THAT WORK

"THE TEACHER SEARCHED TO FIND JUST THE RIGHT WORDS,
AND WHAT HE WROTE WAS UPRIGHT AND TRUE."

Ecclesiastes 12: 10

*H*AVE YOU EVER FELT REALLY tongue-tied? It's horrid to feel really inadequate, overwhelmed with a "word task". Have you ever faced an angry teenager, a hostile workmate? Are you a teacher, Bible Study leader, or small group facilitator? Have you ever had to find words that work?

I had a chance to talk to a large group of people, but there wasn't enough time to prepare. I was scared. There would be doctors and politicians there, PhDs and rich people. Self-important folk, a handful of people who believed like I did, and some who didn't believe much of anything. I began to think of all the people whom I could recommend to do the job.

I felt miserable about declining the invitation, but I thought it would be best for the people inviting me. After all, I wasn't bright enough, I didn't know enough, I wasn't trained enough and I didn't have time enough to put a good talk together! They wouldn't listen to me, I decided.

Before I wrote the letter declining the invitation, I decided

BEFORE I WROTE

THE LETTER

DECLINING THE

INVITATION,

I DECIDED I'D BETTER

CHECK IT OUT

WITH THE LORD.

I'd better check it out with the Lord, even though I was reluctant, anticipating what He might say.

I ran to The Front Door. I was breathless when I arrived. He had seen me coming and He was waiting.

"Catch your breath," He said smiling.

"I've decided to say 'no'," I announced.

"Then why did you come here?"

"I know I shouldn't say yes or no without checking with You," I replied, self-righteously.

"Why are you going to say no?" He asked. I knew He knew the answer.

"I feel so inadequate – and I don't have time."

"Worship Me," He said unexpectedly.

"But I have to go – "

"Worship Me."

I stilled then, pulling my rushing soul up with a jerk.

"All right."

I knelt at His feet. My soul kept looking at its watch! I couldn't concentrate. I felt badly about it. "I don't know how to focus at the moment, Lord," I said. "I know You think I should do it – that's why I thought twice about coming to ask You!"

"You sound a bit like Jonah to me," He said with a laugh.

"Well, I don't want to spend time in the big fish!" I replied. "But I am struggling with the word thing. How do I worship You when my mind keeps forming sentences, and trying to think of illustrations?"

"Worship Me!"

And so I did. I took a little while, but then it was done. My words nestled down at His feet and I began to worship Him there. Then a wonderful thing happened. The words I was using to worship Him kept coming, along with new ideas. These were words and ideas I'd never had before! Suddenly I realized they were perfect for the clever people, and the high and mighty people, and even the clever worldly-wise people I would be talking to!

What's more, somehow I knew my words had wings! It had happened! I knew I had my talk. It would be a talk that would wing its way to many a heart.

Reading me, He said, "These words will fly high and bend low. They will race to the hearts of men and women ahead of other worldly words. They will find their target. They will honour Me, and they will work! My child, words that have first worshipped, will always work."

Then He was gone, and I lingered even though I needed to go. I noticed the heavenly pencil and notepaper He had left behind, so I thought I would leave Him a little note – I sort of turned it into a prayer. It said:

Give my words wings, Lord,
May they fly high enough to reach the mighty,
Low enough to breathe the breath of sweet encouragement
    upon the downcast soul.
Give my words wings, Lord,
May they fly swift and far,
Winning the race with the words of the worldly wise
To the hearts of men.
Give my words wings, Lord,
See them now, nesting down at Your feet,
Silenced into ecstasy,
Home at last.

Lord, help me to remember that words that have worshipped are words that must work! I need always to run to The Front Door before I say yes or no to an invitation to speak or teach. May Your Spirit then always give my words wings. Thank You, Jill.

I keep this prayer in my heart. I use it nearly every day! You can borrow it if you like. Help yourself!

GOD'S FRONT DOOR

THE WELL OF MY WANTING

"IF YOU KNEW THE GIFT OF GOD AND WHO IT IS THAT ASKS YOU
FOR A DRINK, YOU WOULD HAVE ASKED HIM AND HE WOULD
HAVE GIVEN YOU LIVING WATER!"
John 4: 10

HAVE YOU EVER BEEN REALLY thirsty? Nothing else
seems to matter. All you can think about is getting a drink. It's like
that when you are thirsty for God.

I had been reading about the woman Jesus met at the well.
She had been so thirsty and so needy, desperate for a drink of the
water of life. I think I understood a little of that. I myself was
feeling very thirsty for Him right then.

I prayed a prayer poem.

Thirsting for a heart that's warm
Thirsting for a mind that's calm,
Thirsting for a rest of soul
Thirsting for a well-worth goal.
Thirsting for a sense of Him
Thirsting for what might have been.

Thirsting, thirsting hear my cry
Fill me Jesus or I die!

Kneeling at the well of grace
Looking into Jesus' face,
At the end and in despair
Cast myself on You in prayer;
Drawing on Your love for me –
Jesus my sufficiency!

I noticed I had the bucket of my needs in my hands. Suddenly He was there!

"See my bucket, Lord, I'm tired of coming to the well of my wantings. I have been drinking at the well of work, knowledge and family. Even the well of faith for faith's sake does not quench the thirst."

He took my bucket away and said, "Draw waters from the wells of salvation and nowhere else."

So I sat down and listened to the One who was the bread and water of life. There I feasted with Him. Then I was ready to go back to my village and tell everyone, "Come see a man – "

Lord, only You can satisfy my soul.

Fill me up, Lord, I pray!

Life and Service

THE PHARISEE IN ME

"LORD, BE MERCIFUL TO ME A SINNER."
Luke 18: 13

═══════ ☙ ═══════

*D*O YOU EVER STRUGGLE WITH pride? With thinking more highly of yourself than you should?

People were saying such nice things to me. I had just addressed an important group of people. It was hard not to like the accolades. "I had been a help – a blessing." Surely it was all right to feel good about that? I thought I had made all the right noises; "I'm so glad I've been a help, etc" – but I thought I'd better check in with the Lord to make sure I was not getting proud.

"Let another praise you and not your own lips," He advised me. "Forbid people to praise you over much, and never take yourself too seriously! After all, what have you got that you did not first receive?"

"I did, Lord," I said smugly – referring to the "Let another praise you" bit. And then, to make sure He had noticed my humility, "I'm working on 'the personal pronoun'". I had thought of that phrase myself and had actually used it in my talk. I thought it was rather good!

"You need to work a little harder," He replied, mildly.

"Oh!" I looked at Him quickly but He was looking into the distance and it was obvious His mind was on more important things. Suddenly He turned to me and looked at me intently.

"Let not your left hand know what your right hand is doing," He instructed me. "Never promote yourself. Work much of My work in secret.

"Why do you want only to do My work in an advisory capacity? When will you get down and get dirty in the ditch without being asked? Why do you want to take all the credit?" I was stunned.

"I hate pride, and self-righteousness above all things," He said simply.

I saw him then as clearly as anything! The Pharisee in me!

He whom my soul loved was gone, but I lingered until the shadows came. I left my penitence on the Front steps in the shape of a poem and returned home, sad. As I walked through the woods I heard my smug (and less than honest) words again, and curled up inside.

"I'm working on the personal pronoun, Lord!" I felt sick! It just wasn't true!

"I'M WORKING ON 'THE PERSONAL PRONOUN'." I HAD THOUGHT OF THAT PHRASE MYSELF AND HAD ACTUALLY USED IT IN MY TALK. I THOUGHT IT WAS RATHER GOOD!

"You need to work a little harder!" He had said. So I went to work.

Dear Lord, I've found within my heart
Someone who's been there from the start;
A prudish person, self-appointed,
Self-sufficient, self-anointed.
Though I a true disciple be,
I've met the Pharisee in me!

Oh Lord, I'll pray hard on my way,
I'll try to do it every day.
A publican to be I'll try
And beat my breast and sigh and cry.
Then maybe those around will see –
Oops – there's the Pharisee in me!

And why should You, the God of Grace,
Be forced to live here face to face,
With him who hung You up to die
Against an angry, anguished sky –
Who pierced Your feet and crowned Your head
Who laughed and left You then for dead?
Forgive me, Lord, I beg of Thee
Deal with the Pharisee in me!

Lord save me from "the Pharisee in me".

Help me to be honest enough to recognize him at once;

to beat my breast and cry;

"God be merciful to me a sinner!"

Only this way can I return to my house justified.

PAIN

AND

LOSS

THE BROKEN WING

"HE TENDS HIS FLOCK LIKE A SHEPHERD;
HE GATHERS THE LAMBS IN HIS ARMS AND
CARRIES THEM CLOSE TO HIS HEART."
Isaiah 40: 11

***

HAS SOMEONE HURT YOU? Rejected you, slandered you? Have you ever had an ache that won't go away? Where do you go to find help? Go to The Front Door – you won't be disappointed!

I hadn't noticed Him sitting there in the shade with a lamb in His arms. I went over to Him and sat down.

"Talk to Me," He said.

"I'm hurt," I answered. "So hurt."

"I know," He said.

"When will it stop hurting?"

"When you walk in The Front Door," He said.

"Your Front Door?" I asked.

"Mine," He answered very quietly. "Talk to Me about the pain." It was then that I saw the lamb in His arms. I hadn't noticed the creature had broken its leg. It looked quite bedraggled, limp and exhausted.

"I had to wait until he was spent and at the point of dea[th]," the Lamb Maker explained. "He had got himself up on a dangerous ledge, and every time I approached him he got agitated and nearly fell off. I had to wait until all his strength was gone. Then I knew he wouldn't struggle any more and I could rescue him."

"Maybe he didn't know it was You," I suggested.

"He knew," He responded.

He put the lamb down in the long grass to rest. I hadn't noticed the bird in His lap. It had a broken wing.

"There are so many things that are broken in the world," I said. The Bird Maker took hold of the little creature and it fluttered and squawked and tried to escape.

"She will have to lie still if she wants Me to mend her," He said.

"How silly the bird is," I murmured.

He looked at me. Just once. Then I knew I had been silly too.

"If I lie still in Your hands and stop squawking, will You heal my broken wing?" I whispered, not daring to look at Him.

There was silence. Then, "Will you lie still in My hands whether I heal you or not?" He asked me very gently.

"I'll try to," I said after a long pause.

Then, "Come here, little girl," He said, and I don't know how it happened but I was in His arms feeling the beat of His broken heart. I understood at last. Only someone with a broken heart would want to mend broken legs and wings.

He had had His heart broken so mine could be mended. And suddenly it didn't matter any more, about my wing. Lying there, I knew there was nowhere else I would rather be in the whole wide world than in His hands. In fact, it occurred to me that if my wing was mended I would fly away. Whatever would I do without His hands on my life? I wasn't sure I wanted that.

ONLY SOMEONE WITH A BROKEN HEART WOULD WANT TO MEND BROKEN LEGS AND WINGS.

"It doesn't matter dear Heart Maker," I said, "You decide." Then I saw Him smile, and suddenly I was as content with the hurt as without it.

The sun went down on the day, and night came. I slept. He didn't, but then He who keeps Israel never does!

Lord, when I'm hurting it's so hard to talk to You.

Like a bird with a broken wing I fight and squawk.

Help me to remember that what is happening to me is no

surprise to You. Help me to believe You are the mender of

everything. May I lie still in Your hands till my spirit is healthy

and whole. And bring me to the point of leaving the healing

to You in Your time, in Your way. You decide.

ALWAYS MISSING SOMEONE

"DEPART FROM ME, I NEVER KNEW YOU."
Matthew 7: 23

O YOU EVER GET REALLY "heart hungry" for the people you love? Maybe your children got divorced and you lost your grandchildren when they moved a continent away. Or your mother died when you were young and you've had a Mother-hole-in-your-heart ever since. Or like me, your work separates you from your loved ones on an ongoing basis. There has always been someone missing in my life.

"I've lived my life always missing someone," I reflected as I said goodbye to my husband one more time and got ready to climb on one more plane for one more flight, for one more engagement.

When I'm down, I start to feel really sorry for myself. I was down that day as I saw my husband off to the back of beyond in Mali, West Africa, and waited for my plane back to the States.

An hour before take-off – after Stuart, who was sick himself, had said goodbye to me – I began to be thoroughly ill. Oh no, not here, not now, I moaned. Bombako airport would not be my first choice of place in which to be thoroughly ill!

I boarded the plane weeping quietly into my coke, and wondered what to do. I could have a pity party all by myself or I could think about Jesus. I struggled. The thing about a pity party is you don't need to go to the trouble of inviting anyone – you can wallow in things all by yourself.

I looked for the steward to hand in my unfinished coke can and a familiar form put His hand on my shoulder. My heart jumped!

"Lord, you've been in Mali?" I began, stopping abruptly at the silliness of that remark. I knew He loved Africa! He sat down beside me.

"I was thinking," I began eagerly, now that I had His full attention. "I seem to have lived my life always missing someone." No answer. Emboldened that I didn't receive a rebuke, I rushed on – "When I was a young mother, I had to keep saying goodbye to Stuart. Remember, Lord? He was away months on end." I looked at Him quickly. As if He didn't know that – He had recruited him for the job!

"Then I began to travel for You, and I had to say goodbye to my kids," I continued, rushing in where angels fear to tread! Silence. "And now I've only been home a few weeks this whole year and I haven't seen our grandkids at all – and I'll miss most of their birthdays." I squeezed my coke can in my anguish and it erupted all over us. "Oh Lord, I'm so sorry."

I SEEM TO HAVE LIVED MY LIFE ALWAYS MISSING SOMEONE.

"I understand," He interrupted the flood of words. "I feel just as you do every one of your 'man' days Jill. I'm always missing someone. I'm missing all the people I died for, who chose not to come home to Me." I was stunned. I'd never thought of that.

"I'm forever saying goodbye forever," He said very quietly. "I have to meet these people from every tribe and tongue and nation as they come through The Front Door, and ask them to leave."

"What!"

"You only have one chance Jill, you know that," He said. "And that chance is in time – just a brief wisp of a thing – a vapour – but time enough to receive forgiveness and the assurance of salvation and the promise of heaven. As they come home to My house, I have to say to so many, 'Depart from Me, I never knew you.'"

I was stunned. He looked very serious. "Everyone comes through death's door, Jill, but not everyone is allowed to stay."

I sat there clutching my coke can, aghast.

"Lord, that's worse than never going through The Front Door at all," I sputtered. "To take one glance at Your Holiness and heaven's glories and then have to leave – forever?"

"Forever," He said, very quietly.

"That must be hell," I said. "To take one good look at You and then never be able to look again." We were silent together as the cabin crew dimmed the lights for the night.

I dried my tears and noticed then He was nowhere to be

seen. I thought of Stuart on a gruelling twelve-hour trip into the bush, not feeling well, and the hot, hard work ahead of him, encouraging God's pastors who lived among the poor, the oppressed and the dying.

Still feeling lousy, I looked ahead to my itinerary for the next three months and forbade myself to start counting up the "goodbyes" that lay ahead. "Lord," I whispered, "what a privilege to share an infinitesimal part of the fellowship of Your sufferings."

Somewhere an echo of a familiar verse came back to me: "For it has been given to you on behalf of Christ not only to believe on Him but also to suffer for Him."

Thank You, Dear Lord,

for the privilege of

trusting me to

experience a tiny part of

Your daily heartache.

Help Stuart and me to

give what we have left

to make as sure as

"we" can, that at least

a few folk will go

through death's door

and not be asked to

leave! Thank You for

trusting us with this.

DON'T WASTE THE PAIN

THE PEOPLE WHO LOVE AND SERVE the Lord suffer physical pain, or emotional pain, relational pain, or congregational pain. They encounter little troubles and big troubles. Does that ever worry you? Do you ever feel that God is standing in the corner of your life with His hands in His pockets? Permitted pain is a problem for our faith sometimes, isn't it?

It's a conversation we need to have with the Lord!

"It's easy to waste the pain that You permit to come into my life, isn't it Lord?"

"None of you can expect to be exempt from trouble and stress, problems and pain," He replied. "I send My rain on the just and the unjust. I do not promise to save you 'from' the pain, but I certainly promise to save you 'in' the pain."

"When the tough tests come my way, I can be so self-absorbed with it, I am paralyzed."

"Personal pain or corporate pain can drown you. Yet you and I need to keep talking when these times come," He said. "Don't shut Me out! You will need to bear private pain publicly and well for all sorts of reasons. People will be watching and you will have a chance to share My help for you. This will encourage them to trust Me too.

Pain and Loss

Don't waste the pain, let it prove you;
Don't stop the tears, let them cleanse you.
Rest, stop the striving, soon you'll be arriving in My arms.
Don't waste the pain, let it drive you deeper into Me –
I'm waiting and you should have come sooner!

(I love the way He speaks in poems sometimes!)

Then He advised me, "Let the pain drive you to Me; first, for your own good. If you learned first to fly to Me, you would discover resources you never knew you had.

"And you will experience My peace, and My grace; My power and My upholding. You will know the unsearchable riches of darkness, and My hand that reaches out to hold you securely. Don't let the pain drive you away from the only source of help that can heal! Allow it to turn you heavenwards," He said.

"Second, you should let the pain drive you to Me for other people's good." Then He told me a story of a little girl who was travelling in a railway carriage. The train had a full load of passengers and the little girl ran happily from one to the next, chattering and laughing. She was the friendliest little girl that you could imagine! The people in the train began to wonder just who she belonged to. First she was sitting on a grandmotherly knee, then playing with a couple of kids the other end of the carriage. From there, she chattered to a young couple, who gave her a sweet. It was hard to tell just who her parents were. Suddenly the train entered a tunnel. The whistle blew and darkness rushed past the windows. The little girl gave a squeal and dashed into the arms of a quiet young man sitting in the corner. Then the mystery was solved. There was no more doubt who she belonged to. She was safe in her father's arms!

I liked that story a lot and asked Him if I could tell it to others. He laughed and said I could.

"So the reason we need to use the pain is to let people see to whom we belong?"

"Yes, Jill. This way they have a living example of where to go when they enter the dark tunnels of life. They see you helped and healed and it gives them hope."

"OK. But You'll have to help me, because I don't like pain!"

"I don't expect you do," He said dryly. "I didn't tell you to like it, I told you not to waste it!"

"OK, I'll try."

"Good," He replied. "Let's pray about it!" With that He shut His eyes and I couldn't quite make out His words. All I know is that I was strangely helped. Life didn't look nearly so bad as I walked down the hill and home!

Lord, help me, strengthen me;

make me strong

when I am weak, and brave when I

am hurting.

Toughen me tenderly,

for Your sake.

HELP

AND

HEALING

A MINISTRY OF TEARS

"NO ONE SAID A WORD TO HIM, BECAUSE THEY
SAW HOW GREAT HIS SUFFERING WAS."
Job 2: 13

*H*AVE YOU EVER WANTED TO comfort someone who has had one terrible thing happen to them after another? Have you held your peace because you are frightened of saying the wrong thing in the face of their extreme pain? How do you comfort Job?

I was in the Middle East and had just been reading the story of Job's friends and how they had come to comfort him for all his great sufferings. I read, "When they saw him… they could hardly recognize him; they began to weep aloud… Then they sat on the ground with him for seven days and seven nights. No one said a word to him, because they saw how great his suffering was" (Job 2: 12–13).

We had just walked over the border from Israel into Jordan a few days previously. I met Him very early in the morning, near the brook Jabbok, where Jacob wrestled with God. I was wrestling with something too.

"I'm not surprised to find You here," I said. "What a beautiful place." He nodded. There was something I couldn't read in his eyes.

LORD, I FEEL NEAR TO
TEARS ALL THE TIME
AS I LISTEN TO
THESE PEOPLE.

"I've been here before," He said quietly.

"I know," I said, "I read about it in Genesis. I can't believe I'm here."

"I'm glad you came. I sent for you to have a ministry of 'Presence'."

"Well that sounds easy, but now we're here it's so hard – there's so much hatred, such a deep divide and so much hostility. And we've left the same deep-seated smouldering animosity of generations behind us in Israel, only a few short miles away."

There was a deep secret silence that circled around my thoughts and held me into the sadness. I knew He was letting me feel an infinitesimal fragment of His sorrow about the situation.

"Lord," I managed after a bit, "I feel near to tears all the time as I listen to these people."

"I do too."

"Lord, I read in Your Word, that things were not much different when You lived outside The Front Door for a moment of our 'man-time', and that You were a 'man of sorrows and acquainted with grief'."

"It killed Me," He said. I thought about that!

After a bit I ventured – "But You were able to speak words of redemption into the situation, to save the world – and anyway, You are God! In the face of their deep distress I feel so little and

75

helpless and – and 'human'. In fact I feel sort of 'unnecessary'! Can I say anything that will help?"

"No."

"I didn't think I could – so – why am I here?"

"Because this is where I want you! Why does there have to be a 'why'? Isn't it reason enough to be where I want you to be, among the people I send you to? You are here to have a ministry of Presence and a ministry of Silence. Listen to them!"

"But," I ventured "when I can't do anything, or say anything, or change anything – isn't that a waste of time?"

"I want you here to 'feel' something! To feel the hatred, and weep."

"I can do that."

"DO IT THEN!"

He left me, and I took my pencil and wrote a reminder to myself for the next time I walked into a desperate place of pain.

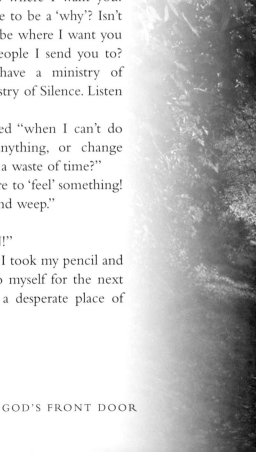

Lord, when there is nothing to do, it seems in the dark day

when pain is so deep and raw around me, and all I can do is to

"be there", listen and weep, remind me it is enough to have a

ministry of presence, a ministry of silence and a ministry of

tears. I can do that Lord, I can do that. Anyone can do that!

Thank You for the privilege.

CRADLE HIM FOR ME

"THE SPIRIT HELPS US IN OUR WEAKNESS.
WE DO NOT KNOW WHAT WE OUGHT TO PRAY FOR,
BUT THE SPIRIT HIMSELF INTERCEDES FOR US,
WITH GROANS THAT WORDS CANNOT EXPRESS."

Romans 8: 26

I RAN TO THE FRONT DOOR. Sitting on the steps, I waited. Today was a terrible day. It was dark and cold outside and the weather matched my heart. He whom I love came quietly outside and sat on the steps beside me.

"Lord, someone I have loved is divorcing our firstborn today."

"I know," He said simply.

"I am in so much emotional pain I can hardly breathe. I can't imagine how our son feels."

"I hate divorce," He said quietly. "I had something better in mind; so much pain." Then he added, "If the Father wills the firstborn drink a cup of sorrow, remember My nail-pierced hands hold the goblet."

He helped me pen a poem after a time, and I gave it to our firstborn later when the dark day was over. He

> I AM IN SO MUCH EMOTIONAL PAIN I CAN HARDLY BREATHE.

helped me put the words on paper wet with tears – and He promised me He would be waiting in the courtroom. He was!

> Dear son, this cup of sorrow
> Must be drunk, it is for thee,
> But be sure He holds the goblet
> Dear son, 'tis He.
>
> Hurting one, he is your Father
> Saw His Son upon the cross,
> Understanding pain and parting
> Knows so well your loss.
>
> Bruised was He but never broken,
> Dim the flax burns in the storm,
> He will strengthen you with power
> He will lead you home.
>
> Firstborn of beloved children
> Joy and pride we have in thee,
> "Father, hear this mother's heartbeat
> Cradle him for me.
>
> "Cradle him for me; cradle him for me,
> Father, hear this mother's heartbeat,
> Cradle him for me!"

Oh my Lord, when I can hardly bear to think about a child's pain, turn me to Yourself. When I cannot see my Bible through my tears, bring scripture to my mind. When I cannot find the right words to pray; pray in me Holy Spirit as You promised with groans which cannot be uttered. Use me to do Your helping and healing work on my knees.

GOD OF THE SECOND CHANCE

GOD IS A GOD OF THE SECOND CHANCE. GOD IS A REDEEMING
GOD. SOMETIMES HE REDEEMS THE MESS AND BRINGS "BEAUTY
FROM ASHES, THE OIL OF JOY FOR MOURNING; THE GARMENT OF
PRAISE FOR THE SPIRIT OF DESPAIR." AND SOMETIMES HE EVEN
"RESTORES THE YEARS THE LOCUSTS HAVE EATEN."

Joel 2: 25 (KJV)

WHAT JOY, YEARS LATER, to pen a wedding poem:

What the locusts have eaten, He's sure to restore,
May the years of your sorrows be remembered no more.
He'll heal and He'll help with your failings and fear
He'll come in the darkness and whisper: "I'm here!"

If you never look back, only ahead,
Keep your eyes on the goal and your soul's heaven-fed,
Your feet on the rock and your heart's in His care
And your arms round each other you'll never despair!

Challenge each other to live for the King,
Spend your lives for Him, and hear your hearts sing,
Serve Him as servants, all of your days,
Honour Him only, in all of your ways.

Parents as parents should parent with grace
As you bring up your children to seek Jesus' face,
Pray for them daily to live after His heart
Then you'll see your prayers answered if you do your part.

Blended and bonded a family again
He'll bind your hearts to Him and heal all your pain,
May you use all your past in the future He's planned
And trust all your present into His able hand!

GOD'S FRONT DOOR

Bless You, Lord, for Your streams of healing and helping grace.

You are surely a redeeming and gracious God. How we praise

You for the balm of Gilead! There is none like You!

$\mathcal{D}$EVOTION

THE DEEP PLACES WHERE
NOBODY GOES

"Do not forsake your friend and
the friend of your father."
Proverbs 27: 10

HAVE YOU BEEN LOOKING for love in all the wrong places? Is there still a deep hunger and longing in your soul to be fulfilled internally in the deep places where nobody goes? Christ by His Spirit can meet that longing. You just have to ask Him.

"Do you remember when all you knew was an intimate loneliness?" He asked me.

We were sitting on The Front Door step, talking. I thought back to the time when my hungering heart and malnourished, empty spirit wondered silently if they would ever experience a dawn chorus.

"Do you remember going to the deep place inside you where nobody goes, where time stands still?"

"And I was suddenly surprised by a familiar stranger?"

"Yes."

"Of course." There was a companionable silence. I remembered the day, marvelling – "How did He get here," and fast upon the heels of that thought, another – "I don't care how He got here, I only want Him to stay forever!" I thought about how the birds sang, angels laughed, and all the trees of the hills clapped their hands. He smiled. I had forgotten He hears my thoughts!

I THOUGHT BACK TO THE TIME WHEN MY HUNGERING HEART AND MALNOURISHED, EMPTY SPIRIT WONDERED SILENTLY IF THEY WOULD EVER EXPERIENCE A DAWN CHORUS.

"Has 'this' familiar stranger become your familiar friend since He met you in the deep places where nobody goes?" He asked me.

"As someone said to me, 'It's easier to be friends with Jesus' friends, than friends with Jesus'," I replied. "Forgive me, Lord."

He took my heart in His hands and kept it very still until it became broken and contrite. Then He kissed my bowed head and mended my spirit. Wordless, I rested against His shoulder in the deep places where nobody goes.

There I revelled in God.

Lord, make me very sure You have not only come to stay in the deep places where nobody goes, but that You feel at home in my heart; that You are celebrated in my Spirit and that You fill my soul full to overflowing with Your love. Thank You for being my dear familiar friend. Love, Jill.

I didn't want to leave. So I stayed a while and thought about
"revelling" in God.

> I revel in Your beauty and I celebrate Your peace
> And as I am obedient I find such sweet release.
> I'm passionate to please You and live a life of praise
> So I'll smile at dark tomorrows and sanctify my days.
>
> Ever climbing upward and reaching for a star,
> I know no sense of loneliness for I know where You are;
> You're living in my ransomed soul, You're filling every day
> So I'll lose myself in loving and I'll give myself away.
>
> I revel in Your presence, and I celebrate Your grace
> And I want to stay forever and look into Your face,
> But now is time for serving and I need to do my part
> So let my tired world see You, reflected in my heart.

89

FIRST WASH ME

"If we confess our sins, He is faithful and
just and will forgive us our sins and purify
us from all unrighteousness."
I John 1: 9

───────── ☙ ─────────

HAVE YOU EVER RUSHED INTO His presence without
washing your feet? Without saying sorry? We don't know enough
about repentance. He would like to teach us! Stop long enough
to hear Him say, "Take off your shoes, for this is holy ground."

I arrived a bit breathless at The Front Door. It was a hot,
dusty day and it seemed the climb up the hill was getting steeper
– or it could be because I had just had another birthday! I
knocked on the door lightly and sat down on the steps to wait.
Nothing happened so I climbed down the steps and began to
walk a little by the River of Repentance that ran alongside The
Front Door.

"Take off your shoes," said a beautiful voice that reminded
me of a waterfall. As I immediately bent to take them off, He
added, "This is holy ground!"

We stood still and I looked at my misshapen feet standing
next to His wonderful, terrible nail-pierced ones.

I noticed then, that my feet badly needed washing. "It's all that dust, Lord," I said apologetically.

"That's what happens when you walk through the world," He replied. "Sit down."

"Uh?"

He took a cloth and wiped my dusty feet. I felt very "Peter like". "Lord," I blurted out, "I feel awkward – dressed, yet strangely naked – humbled."

He didn't answer. I knew then what He was saying without words. I needed the dirt of the world washing off me before we could meet and talk business. His business. I looked at my clean feet. Funny things, but ready now to be shod with the gospel shoes He wanted me to wear.

All right, Lord, I understand
You can't wash my feet if I am wearing sin's sandals.
 See – bare feet!
I'm standing still now on holy ground.
Somehow it's hard to trample
all over other people's lives
with bare feet, Lord.

I feel awkward like this;
Dressed, yet naked, humbled –
Bare feet!
Funny things –
but ready to be shod
with the gospel shoes You would give me to wear,

But first, Lord,
wash me!

Lord, teach me to pause here always to say: "First wash me!" I rush around Your world at such a pace. I tramp through the dusty streets without first having my feet shod with the preparation of the gospel of peace. Teach me to say: "First wash me." Then it will be time to go and find the needy ones, to tell them where they can find cleansing too.

SHADOW ME

I'M SO THIRSTY, FATHER. It's awfully hot outside The Front Door. It feels as if I'm living in a desert!

"You are. You are living in a hot and weary land. I will refresh you. Look around, what do you see?"

"A river."

"Drink deeply."

"Thank You, Father."

"You're welcome. Look around, what else do you see?"

"A shadow."

"It's Me."

"Oh, You look like a rock."

"I am."

"You are Rock and Shadow?"

"Yes. A shadow is an inescapable companion. But stay by me, Jill. Stay in My shadow. There is refreshing grace for all your needs at My side."

Then I entered the shadow and everything was beautiful. Rainbows chased each other around and I felt the sprinkling of life-giving water on my face.

"Where did You get all this refreshing grace, Father?"

"I Am."

"Yes, I know. I need to show more grace. But I'm me and You are You."

"Yes. Show more of Me."

"How?"

"Just stay near me. Live in My shadow. Shadow Me."

"I can do that."

"What's a shadow, Jill?"

"The reality to the substance?"

"Correct. Think of a great rock in the middle of a desert. Imagine the searing sun, and the sizzling sand. Then the sun goes down and the cool shadow of the rock grows."

"I know what You are going to say."

"What?"

"You are like the shadow of a mighty rock within a weary land."

"Yes, but you can be too."

"Me?"

"Yes, you. You can both live 'in' My

THEN I ENTERED THE SHADOW AND EVERYTHING WAS BEAUTIFUL.

shadow and 'be' My shadow. Remember, a shadow is an inescapable companion."

"It is attached to the Rock?"

"Exactly."

"That's why You said I should 'stay close'?"

"Yes. Then you will show more grace."

"Oh Father, I will, I will. I know what You mean; spend much time in secret with You alone, but sometimes it's hard to stay close to You outside The Front Door."

"That's up to you."

"Yes, Lord… "

"What is it?"

"Give me Grace to do it."

"I will. I Am."

Then I heard Him say very clearly again, "SHADOW ME."

Oh Father, I am harsh and unkind. You are gentle and loving.
Help me to rise early and retire late. May I insist on
"shadowing You" till I really know what it means to be Your
inescapable companion. Refresh me that I may refresh others.
May many seek the cool refreshing shade of my life.

WAN-A-PIECE-OF-ME?

"How great is the love the Father has lavished on us,
that we should be called children of God."
I John 3: 1

━━━━━━━━━━━━━ ❧ ━━━━━━━━━━━━━

*D*O YOU EVER WONDER what the Father thinks about you? Does He think you are a cute kid even when you are naughty?

I was sitting on The Front Door steps talking to Him about our visit to Texas.

"Our grandkids are growing up so fast."

"It happens."

"Liam is so cute," I gushed. "Even when he's naughty. I could eat him with a spoon, as they say in England!" He laughed.

"They don't have that saying in Texas," I went on (as if He didn't know). "They say, 'I wan-a-piece of you!'"

"Same thing," He smiled.

AFTER ANOTHER QUIET INTERLUDE, I SAID, "LORD I THINK YOU HAVE ALL OF ME."

"Liam has all these doting mothers at church saying to him, 'I wan-a-piece of you.' So he runs around with that cute grin asking everyone, 'Do you wan-a-piece of me?' It's so sweet!" There was silence then as we thought about it.

"I don't wan-a-piece of you," He said after a bit.

"You don't?" I asked, my heart beginning to beat.

"No, I want 'all' of you," He said quietly.

"Oh."

After another quiet interlude, I said, "Lord I think You have all of me."

"Yes, I do," He said.

"You are amazing," I said. "And I'm not even cute, in fact I'm not very nice at all!"

Then, because He waited, I was able to say – right to His face, "Lord, thank You for wanting my everything, even when I am a downright unpleasant kid; not a nice child at all. You are the best!"

Maybe you feel the same as I did – such love! Why don't you thank Him too?

TRUST
AND
FAITH

TRUST ME

*I*S THE WORLD IN WHICH WE LIVE scaring you? It's a pretty scary place at the moment. On the eve of war with Iraq the news was ominous. I wanted to gather our kids and grandkids under my wings, run home and hide under the bed.

I was sitting by The Front Door reading the newspaper. I felt relieved when He sat down beside me. "Look at this; a war may break out Lord, today or tomorrow or certainly by the end of the week, a real live war – a terrible war."

"I read it before they wrote it," He commented briefly. His face was grave. That scared me.

"It's Pete's birthday today," I said. "He's 40."

"I remember," He said.

"So do I," I said with feeling. We laughed.

"But Lord, he's in the prime of life, and his ministry has taken off," I stopped. I had just remembered He was 33 when He 'finished' His work! Pete had already had seven more years than the Lord!

"What does the future look like for our children and their children? I seem to see nothing but mushroom clouds and people hobbling about without limbs, looking at the world with one eye! I feel I'm living in a world being driven by a very drunk driver," I said.

I FEEL I'M LIVING

IN A WORLD BEING

DRIVEN BY

A VERY

DRUNK DRIVER.

He had stayed quite still. Now He spoke – "Why are you bothered? Why don't you trust Me? This world is not your home."

"But I want my children and grandkids to have a long life – "

"They will."

"But not if there's a war."

"They will all have a very long life," He reminded me. "Eternally long!"

"But Lord, there's so much unfinished business."

"Like what?"

"Well, there's so much conflict in the world, and in the church too. People biting at, and devouring each other… "

"I remember when My own disciples were at each other all the time, fussing and arguing. I said to them, 'Have salt in yourselves and be at peace with each other – what are you arguing about?' "

"Did it bother You?"

"Yes, it bothered Me."

103

I was quiet for a bit, thinking. I thought about how He had spent His last incredibly precious moments in the upper room praying that this rambunctious crew of disparate people would live in peace with one another. Unity and harmony were obviously very important to Him.

"It worked out," He said briefly, following my train of thought. "My people are to be peace makers."

"But sometimes war is inevitable?" I asked.

"Sometimes war is inevitable," He replied. "With nations and with individuals. So it will be till I come again." Then I remembered He had said there would be wars and rumours of wars till the end came.

"Lord, sometimes I'm more bothered by disagreements in the family or Your family, the church, than I am about wider hostility and conflicts abroad."

He gave me a little thought to write in my Bible.

"Lord, let me learn to let it bother You, and refuse to let it bother me."

I read it out loud before I began my duties for the day for a week or two. War or no war, this is what trust is about.

Lord God, who sent Your Son to be our peace;
may we be His agents of blessing and reconciliation in
a desperate and dying world.

WHEN FAITH SEES FEAR COMING

"PERFECT LOVE DRIVES OUT FEAR,
BECAUSE FEAR HAS TO DO WITH PUNISHMENT."
I John 4:18

───────────── ❧ ─────────────

ARE YOU A FEARFUL PERSON? There is surely enough to be frightened of in our fallen world. Fear comes in all sorts of shapes and sizes. It can suddenly sneak up on you unexpectedly like a terrorist, or with ominous warning signals like a siren or the drone of an aeroplane. Fear can make you ill; cause heart attacks, or fainting spells. I hate the sick feelings of fear. Jesus said, "Perfect love casts out fear," so I went to talk to "Perfect Love" about it!

"Lord, You are bigger than all my fears and phobias," I told Him. "But even though I believe that, I am still frightened!"

"It's not My will that My children should live in fear," He replied. I wondered silently then how many years I had spent living outside

FAITH IN A GOD
BIG ENOUGH,
AND NEAR ENOUGH, AND
POWERFUL ENOUGH TO
TEACH ME
HOW TO TRUST AND NOT
BE AFRAID.

of His will! I had spent much of my life living scared. We began to talk of the way, over the years, He had helped me to overcome many of my fears, fears that had buried me in the past. If I had overcome some, then why not others?

"If you fear God you have nothing else to fear," Jesus reminded me. "Don't fear him who can kill the body! Fear him who has the power to cast both body and soul into hell. The devil is the father of fear whereas God is the Father of faith."

"The fear of death is a biggie, isn't it, Lord? You remember, I know, how flying nearly grounded me as a speaker! How could I get on a plane in a total panic and then get off and start speaking about faith? Then You gave me real victory in this area of my life – maybe that's because You gave me lots of practice!"

"I noticed that you just got your 100,000-mile frequent flyer card for actual miles flown in one year. Well done!" He commented.

"Well, it's been faith that has chased my fears away! Faith in a God big enough, and near enough, and powerful enough to teach me how to trust and not be afraid."

There was a long silence. We were both thinking about the same thing!

"How come I still have so many obsessive fears?"

"How come indeed?"

"I don't know – as soon as I get over one thing there are a hundred other things waiting for me to be afraid of, waiting to step into line!"

"Start by thanking Me for all the fears I 'have' overcome for you, Jill. This will give you confidence."

"Oh Lord, I feel terrible. Like the nine lepers who forgot to come back and say thank you!"

"Say it now."

"All right. Do You remember how I hated to be laughed at ever since I was a little girl?"

"Well, you were really shy growing up and used to blush all the time. Then you became My child who must stand up and speak out, and that took care of your self-consciousness in a hurry!"

"Thank You for making me a witness to You! You helped me with my inordinate fear of loneliness too, Lord. You knew I would spend a good part of many years being apart from Stuart, and that was where I learned to lean on You!"

"It taught you not to treat your husband like the Holy Spirit!" He replied.

"Thank You Lord! Then there was the fear that my children would not make it with God. Don't You remember my inordinate fear that they wouldn't make it spiritually; that they would grow up to resent the time we spent on other people's kids in ministry?"

"You had to learn to let that go, and promise Me you would go on with Me even if your children didn't."

"That was hard!"

"Yes. But once said and meant, it dealt with the fear, didn't it?"

"Truly it did!"

"Jill, when fear sees faith coming it trembles. It knows its days are numbered. Where is your faith?"

That was the question. Where was it? I had enough evidence of

WHY WAS THIS PUNISHING FEAR FOR MY CHILDREN, AND THEIR CHILDREN, OUR HEALTH AND WELFARE, OUR INTER-PERSONAL RELATIONSHIPS WITHIN THE FAMILY, OUR MINISTRY OPPORTUNITIES, STILL ABLE ALMOST TO PARALYZE ME?

109

His power over fear in my past to care for all the fears in the present and future, but where was it? Why was this punishing fear for my children, and their children (it never seems to stop), our health and welfare, our inter-personal relationships within the family, our ministry opportunities, still able almost to paralyze me?

"Remember," I heard Him say as He went through The Front Door, "There is no fear in love, but perfect love drives out fear because fear has to do with punishment!"

It was late in the day. I didn't want to go home and deal with two of my favourite fears crouching on the doorstep waiting for me there. So I lingered, playing with words on a bit of paper, catching our conversation in a favourite way He had given me so I could remember His advice.

When fear sees faith a-coming, when doubt sees truth
    displayed,
With the truth that is in Jesus, how can I be dismayed?
When tears are wept in secret, when sorrow's night
    descends,
Then faith in Jesus' power my sorry soul defends.

When I am busy drowning in a sea of deep despair,
When those I love have hurt me and my soul needs God's
    repair,
When loneliness o'erwhelms me with an ache that none can
    touch;
And I'm crushed with disappointments, and life is just too
    much.

When danger threatens loved ones; when death stalks near to
    home;
When war shall rise against me; when panic's on the throne;
Remind me of Your promises, renew my heart in grace
And help me live in righteousness and truth before Your
    face.

So Jesus be my comfort and remind me in Your Word
That our small voice in the tempest incredibly is heard,
In the heaven You inhabit, in the Love Land where You live
As You travel through the universe Your peace to me to give!

So I wait now in this stillness that garrisons my soul.
Yes, I wait with hands uplifted till You come and make me
    whole,
So when faith sees fear a-coming to fill my heart with
    dread
Oh Lord Jesus great and mighty, will You please kill fear
    dead?

Trust and Faith

Lord, You remind me in Your Word: "When they were overwhelmed with dread, there was nothing to dread!" Help me to use the shield of faith and the sword of the Spirit which is the Word of God, to put doubt and despair behind me. Lord, increase my faith.

$\mathcal{H}$EAVEN

PEGGY

HAVE YOU SUFFERED LOSS? Did your wife or husband leave you? Did a sibling die? Death appears so final, doesn't it? It leaves you with an intimate loneliness that only God can touch.

Someone I loved deeply had just walked through The Front Door. I talked to the Lord about it. He told me to read the story of the raising of Lazarus. I read: "Take off the grave clothes and let him go."

He didn't wait for me to come to The Front Door. He met me in the pew in church, sitting looking at that box with Peggy's remains inside.

"Lord," I whispered, "I was there when my Peggy went through The Front Door."

"I know, I saw you there, sitting by her side, holding her hand."

"Suddenly the room was all light and airy as if Your breath blew into the stuffy death chamber."

"Angels' wings," He said without any explanation. But I knew it anyway. You know when it happens.

"Were You there?" I asked. I knew the answer before He spoke.

"I opened the door," He said simply.

"I knew it was You," I blurted out breathlessly. "I was reading about Lazarus and just as I got to the bit when You said, 'Lazarus, come forth', I looked up because…"

"Because you heard Me, didn't you, Jill?"

"Yes, Lord," I whispered.

"Did you hear Me tell the angels 'Loose her and let her go'?" He asked me. I couldn't answer – too many scalding tears were running down my face. He put them in His bottle to carry them away.

"Precious tears, precious Peggy, precious Jill," I heard Him say. "I lost a mother once," He said quietly. "It was Me who had to go through The Front Door first. Not the usual way it happens!"

"I know," I said.

"It was hard watching her watching Me. I couldn't put My arms around her. They were pinned quite securely in place."

"So You could open The Front Door for her one day?"

"Yes."

"Thank You."

"You will see Peggy soon, you know. When it's time, I'll bring her with Me – to The Front Door to meet you."

I couldn't speak again, but then I didn't have to. He understood.

Lord, thank You that there is a Front Door to go through.
We take so much for granted, those of us who have grown up
knowing about it all. Then someone we love so much we can't
breathe goes through it. Then and only then do we really begin
to be thankful for the fact that there is a door to go through at
all! And, Oh dear Lord, thank You that You opened it with Your
nail-pierced hand. That must have hurt – so much!
Thank You, thank You, thank You! Oh and thank You for
promising to bring Peggy to The Front Door to meet me.
That helps. I love You, Jesus.

GOD'S FRONT DOOR

HEAVEN

AFTER SITTING ON THE STEPS for a while, I made up a little poem to help me remember the things I had glimpsed when He had let me peek through The Front Door. Here it is. You could write one too –

HEAVEN

What place is this where rivers flow
And flowers bud and grasses grow?
Where birds compete to praise God's Son,
Where prayers are answered every one.

What place is this where minds released
From fear and phobia find peace?
Where constant joy is all I know,
Where God is everywhere I go,
Where I am overwhelmed to see
The face of Him who died for me!

What place is this where tears are dried
By hands of Jesus crucified?
Where broken dreams are dreamt anew
And come to pass for me, for you.
What place, what place, but home to Him
Who'll make me what I might have been.

Then I will praise Him all my days
And know that He accepts my praise.
What place is this? It's heaven to be
At home for all eternity!

EVERLAND

"IN MY FATHER'S HOUSE ARE MANY ROOMS;
IF IT WERE NOT SO, I WOULD HAVE TOLD YOU."
John 14: 2

⸙

Do you ever wonder what heaven is like? The time for finding out is before you get there! The Bible tells us much about it.

It was evening and I was falling asleep. I was wondering where Peggy was living in Everland. She had had a lovely house here, but I was sure it wasn't nearly as beautiful as the one up there. I wondered if she had a garden. She loved her roses so. I remembered Jesus talked about houses in Everland to His disciples one day. Before I went to sleep I stopped by The Front Door.

"I have a lovely home," He reminded me. I knew He would have. How could it be otherwise?

"Lord of Glory," I heard myself ask, "What is Your house like? Does it stand in a garden?"

"Watch carefully and I'll open The Front Door for a few minutes so you can look through. There, what do you see?"

"Oh, great Lord of Everland, it's so beautiful! I see flowers that never fade, trees that are laden with fruit, and light that never dims."

"What do you hear?"

"I hear birds that never stop singing and laughter that sounds like a thousand rivers." I noticed then that the laughter came from people who live for ever.

I HEAR BIRDS THAT NEVER STOP SINGING AND LAUGHTER THAT SOUNDS LIKE A THOUSAND RIVERS.

"Can you see the angels?"

"I don't know, yet I think I feel the brush of their wings! Oh, Lord of Everland, how long will it be till we move house? Till we will all be there?"

"Soon, very soon. And you will be there as long as I am," He answered. Then I was satisfied and He closed The Front Door and kissed me asleep.

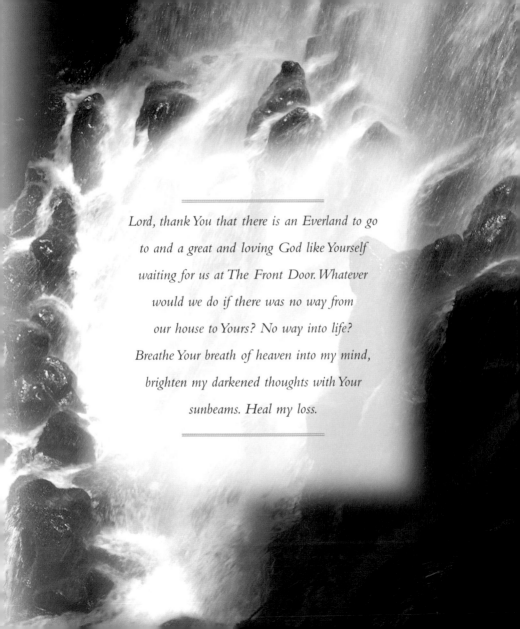

Lord, thank You that there is an Everland to go

to and a great and loving God like Yourself

waiting for us at The Front Door. Whatever

would we do if there was no way from

our house to Yours? No way into life?

Breathe Your breath of heaven into my mind,

brighten my darkened thoughts with Your

sunbeams. Heal my loss.

CHRISTMAS
AND
EASTER

The crib is incredible, the cross indescribable, and the cave indispensable with its message of hope for a dying and desperate planet full of people who cannot forgive their own sins, keep themselves alive, or raise themselves from the dead. The empty cave is the reason my life is so full today. Full of life and audacious laughing faith in the glorious God of Christmas morning, Easter Sunday and the miracle of Pentecost!

WHERE WERE YOU GOING?

———— ❦ ————

"**W**HERE WERE YOU GOING WHEN You left heaven, Lord? To Bethlehem or Nazareth? To fair Galilee or Royal Jerusalem? To cross or tomb? Where were You going on Christmas night, to heaven's portals? To the throne of grace?"

"Nay, child: just passing through! On Christmas night I was coming to you! This, this, this, was where I was going!"

Hay in His hair and stars in His eyes,
cradled in crib, and quiet He lies.
What does He know, and who does He see –
needy humanity like you and me?

Dust in His sandals, chisel in hand,
building a fine house in Nazareth land.
What is He thinking; what's on His mind –
is He mourning the family He'll soon leave behind?

Stone for His pillow, a travelling man,
healing and helping, preaching God's plan,
proving His deity, rejected by those
who should have known better than to be His foes.

Cross on His shoulder, thorns on His brow,
whipped like a dog and kicked like a cow,
slapped by tormentors, tortured and torn –
dear God, was He sorry He'd ever been born?

Early one morning, long before dawn,
folding the grave clothes He'd worn for His own,
rising to bless us and willing to come
into our poor hearts to call them His home.

Spirit abundant, life from the tomb,
bursting earth's barriers into this room,
we'll live for Your pleasure – oh bless with Your smile –
may our dedication make Calvary worthwhile.

Lord Jesus Christ, Thank You for breaking Your Father's heart to mend mine. Thank You for making that great graph of grace from highest heaven to earth in order to take me home. Help me to tell Your lost world!

GOD'S FRONT DOOR

WHATEVER IT TAKES

⸻ ❧ ⸻

IT WAS THE CHRISTMAS SEASON and I was thinking about all the tinsel triviality around me. The Grinch was winning big time! I had been frantically rushing around my world in ever-decreasing circles. Have you ever been like this at Christmas? So hectic that you miss what it's all about? I was sitting on The Front Door step at last, when it opened and He whom my soul loves joined me.

"Lord," I began as my soul stopped rushing around inside me and sat down for a few saving moments – "Speak to me. Do whatever it takes to touch the quiet place within me where You live. Whatever it takes, Lord, do what it takes to renew my faith and set my spirit dancing, so I can do whatever it takes to tell my world why You came at Christmas." He smiled at me thoughtfully as if remembering something. Then He spoke.

> LORD, SPEAK TO ME. DO WHATEVER IT TAKES TO TOUCH THE QUIET PLACE WITHIN ME WHERE YOU LIVE.

"One day I said to my Father, 'Whatever it takes Father, I'll do it. Whatever it takes to bring them all home to our house.' And my Father said to me: 'Go to Bethlehem! That's what it takes!' And so I came! As a baby, born to a woman who barely counted her age in double figures. Go to Bethlehem, Jill."

I KNEW AT ONCE WHAT HE WAS TELLING ME. I NEEDED TO GO TO BETHLEHEM.

I knew at once what He was telling me. I needed to go to Bethlehem. I had been to the mall, to the outlets, to visit the family, but I hadn't been to Bethlehem! I had fallen foul of the Christmas rush. I went – right then and there. You can too, you know. It changed my Christmas. It will change yours!

======

Lord, I worship You, I am in awe! I am reduced in spirit, Lord, overcome with remorse that I have for far too long allowed my faith to lie low at Christmas of all times! I have allowed the Grinch to steal my Christmas. Forgive me!

======

THE CROSS

ANOTHER GOOD FRIDAY. Time to wonder anew at the price of my redemption. Oh God, only through the cross can we enter heaven. Don't let me ever forget it!

Shadows dress Him like a shroud
Stones that watch Him cry out loud;
Trees a thousand years in age
Bow their heads in silent rage.

Earth refreshed by Jesus' grief
Quakes in angry unbelief.
Birds restrain their song in awe
Little creatures play no more.
All creation holds its breath
As He who gave life faces death!

See Him now –
A broken-hearted Christ upon a cross, bent in the shape of
    my sin.
Eternity's vaults emptied of their greatest treasure,

Aching with the pain of purchase,
Wait for the long journey down, down and down to be
    done!

Darkened with death's breath, the world waits.

God's Child arched in agony refuses to stop loving us all.
Wrapped in swathing bands of pain,
Careless of hell's happiness, He hangs, He hurts, He dies.

After penning my thoughts, I looked at The Front Door. Why
had I never noticed it before? It was in the shape of a cross!

Christmas and Easter

Lord, only through the cross can I enter; only through the cross am I saved. You are the door of the sheepfold. Thank You. Your loving child, Jill.

GOOD FRIDAY

"THEY LED HIM OUT TO CRUCIFY HIM."
Mark 15: 20

"**E**ASTER COMES AROUND as quickly as Christmas, Lord, or so it seems," I murmured as I slipped into a back pew.

"Yes."

"I'm glad so many people come to Good Friday services. I'm glad I can be here." Silence.

"I'm trying to concentrate Lord; to focus on what it's all about."

"It's hard for you when you're so worried about your son," He said simply.

"Yes."

I tried and tried to keep my mind on the service, but at the end of the day there I was worrying myself into a state. The last hymn was announced and I gave a guilty start.

"Lord, forgive me," I cried in the deep chamber of my soul. "I feel terrible. I couldn't concentrate. In fact, I may as well not have been here. You see my son is in trouble, he's dying inside."

Then I heard sweet understanding saying to my soul,

"When My Son was dying I couldn't think about anything else either, so I understand, and My Son was dying on the inside and the outside!"

Then I sat quietly till all the people left the sanctuary and thought about the day His Son came home through The Front Door, all bloodied and beaten up, and I wept. "I'm sorry Father, I'm so sorry Father, for my part. Forgive me."

"Done," I heard Him say. "See you on Resurrection morning!"

Father, thank You for Good Friday. Never let me get used to

the things I know, or distracted by the things You allow.

Keep the cross before me all the days of my life!

LIGHT ARISING

Light arising, God surprising
Children locked in night,
Resurrection power displaying
All Your glorious light.
Surely, Lord, this tomb of trouble
Deep within my soul
Needs a visit, love exquisite,
Healing till it's whole!

See my heart, all, not in part,
Filled with doubt and dread –
I hurt, I cry, and You know why
It's what's been done and said:
The power to be like You Yourself,
To let the grievance go.
It's up to love to rise above
This trouble down below!

It's hard to live, to love, and give
Forgiveness for a wrong,
But Jesus, see a broken me
Who so much needs Your song!

Oh Father, know that as I go
To mend and do my part,
I'll ask for power in this sad hour
To heal a broken heart.

Light arising, God surprising
Children of the Lord,
Hearts are cold and love's grown old
And needs to be restored.
This Easter day, Lord, come what may
Remove this mighty stone
Of hurt and grief, bring sweet relief –
Reign, Lord, and reign alone.

Light arising, God surprising
Children of the cross.
Newness making, now forsaking
All our pain and loss.
Jesus love me, heal me, help me,
Send me to Your own
To tell the power in this dark hour
That Christ is on His throne!

Christmas and Easter

Jill Briscoe and her husband Stuart live in
Milwaukee, Wisconsin. They have worked
together for over 40 years, and have three
grown children and thirteen grandchildren.
A native of Liverpool, Jill is a prolific
writer. She serves on the board of directors
of World Relief and of *Christianity Today*,
and is a popular speaker at key Christian
events around the world.